They Fought for Freedom

Ruth First

D1827625

Don Pinnock

Series Editor: John Pampallis
Consulting Editor: Chris van Wyk

Maskew Miller Longman

Maskew Miller Longman (Pty) Ltd
Howard Drive, Pinelands, Cape Town

Offices in Johannesburg, Durban, Port Elizabeth, Kimberley,
King William's Town, Pietersburg, Nelspruit, Umtata and Mafikeng,
and representatives throughout southern Africa.

First published 1995

ISBN 0 636 01954 3

Map by Anne Westoby
Set in 11 on 13 pt Sabon
Typesetting and layout by Beverley Visser
Imagesetting and scanning by Den Graphics
Printed by CTP Book Printers (Pty) Ltd
Caxton Street, Parow 7500, Cape Town

RM3864

Acknowledgements

The author and publisher would like to thank the following individuals for their help
and guidance:

Tilly First, Joe Slovo, Gillian Slovo, Robyn Slovo, Dr John Daniels, Prof. Gavin
Williams, Dr Andre Odendaal and Patricia Pinnock.

The publisher is indebted to the following organisations for photographs, illustrations
and other archival material:

The Mayibuye Centre and the Archives, Institute for Historical Research at the
University of the Western Cape, Bellville; the South African Library and *Sunday Times*.

Every effort has been made to trace the owners of copyright material, but in some
cases this has not been possible. The publisher would be glad to hear from any further
copyright owners so that appropriate arrangements can be made.

Other books in this series:

Steve Biko	Yusuf Dadoo	Seretse Khama
Z K Matthews	Sol Plaatje	Mohandas Gandhi
Chris Hani	Oliver Tambo	Dora Tamana

Titles in preparation:

Abdul Abdurahman	James la Guma	Helen Joseph	Bram Fischer
Edwin Mofutsanyana	Albert Luthuli	Joe Slovo	John Dube
Matthew Goniwe	James Calata	Lillian Ngoyi	Cissie Gool
Dorothy Zihlangu			

Contents

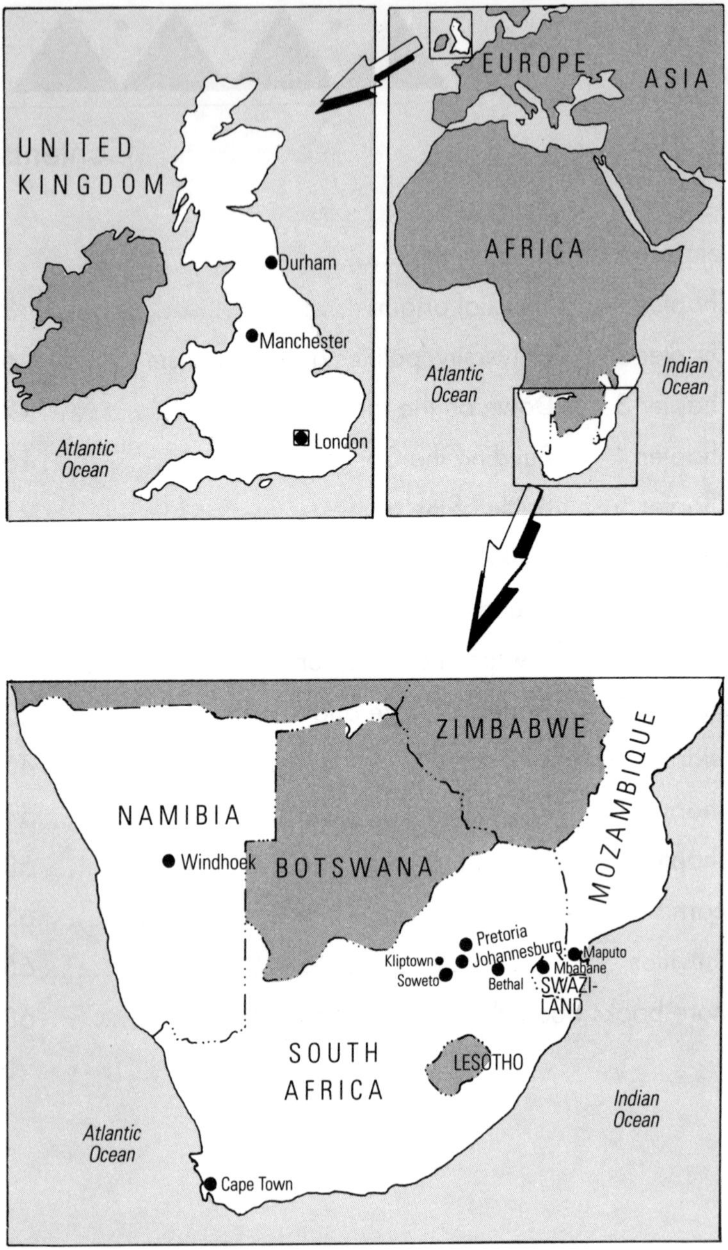

Important places in Ruth First's life

Before we begin our story

Tuesday afternoon, 4.30 pm, 17 August 1982. Ruth First was in her office at Eduardo Mondlane University in Maputo where she worked as Director of Research at the Centre for African Studies. With her were her closest friend Bridget O'Laughlin, the Centre's director, Aquino de Bragança, and a South African exile, Pallo Jordan. They were all talking excitedly about the conference Ruth had helped to organise the previous week.

The conference had looked at the problems which Mozambique was having because it was so close to racist South Africa. The delegates had discussed how academics could play a part in solving these problems.

Ruth was at her desk, going through her incoming post while she talked and laughed. She picked up a small parcel and cut it open. Suddenly a terrific explosion ripped through the office. Windows shattered, a hole was torn in the wall and the steel desk snapped in half like a toy. The concrete ceiling cracked down the middle. Bridget, Aquino and Pallo were injured. But Ruth, who was bending over the desk, took the full force of the blast and was killed.

The parcel bomb that killed her sent shock waves around the world. In South Africa, however, the news of her death was hardly mentioned in the press. At her funeral in Llanguene Cemetery near Maputo the following Monday, 3 000 mourners gathered around Ruth's coffin which was covered with the flag of the African National Congress. There were workers and students as well as the prime ministers and ambassadors from many countries. At the graveside the ANC Women's

The "ideas that mattered to her most were those that were instruments* in the liberation of people. She was warm and sensitive. And she was such fun."

—Ronald Segal

League described her as a fighting woman. ANC secretary general, Alfred Nzo, said she was an inspiration and an encouragement. Umkhonto weSizwe, the military wing of the ANC, pledged to avenge her death. The president of Mozambique, Samora Machel, said her ideals were also the ideals of his country, and Sam Nujoma, who was to become president of Namibia, called her a heroine. Messages of sympathy poured in from 67 countries and organisations, adding to the letters and telegrams from hundreds of friends throughout the world.

As Ruth's coffin was lowered into the grave, voices rose up in the old song of the socialist movement, *The Red Flag.*

The president of the ANC, Oliver Tambo, wrote to Ruth's husband, Joe Slovo, and her children. He said Ruth's life story was a record of achievement. This book tells the story of that achievement.

---

* *All words with an asterisk like this can be found in the section "Learn new words" at the back of the book.*

Unusual origins

Ruth First was born in 1925. Her family was white and lived in a comfortable house in Johannesburg. Yet in almost every way her family was different to its neighbours. This was to make Ruth's path through life different to that of most white South Africans. Her grandparents were Jews who had to flee from Russia because of the terrible brutality known as the pogroms*. These people carried with them to South Africa the memories of what it was like to be poor and persecuted. And they never forgot.

The pogroms were attacks on Jews. Jewish families were not liked in Russia. They lived in very poor conditions and were only allowed to stay in a "homeland" called the Pale of Settlement. There was overcrowding and great poverty.

In 1881 the Russian leader, Tsar Alexander the Second, was killed by an assassin and Jews were blamed. A wave of anti-Jewish pogroms spread through the Pale of Settlement. Jews were made out to be dangerous revolutionaries. They began leaving Russia and within three years a huge Jewish migration had begun. Over the next thirty years, sixteen million Jews moved from Eastern Russia to the United States. In only one year, 1903, more than 70 000 people from Europe came to live in South Africa.

Among these immigrants were Ruth's grandparents. They had heard that the streets of Johannesburg were paved with gold, and they came to make a new life. But in Johannesburg they found more dust than gold. And it was hot and dry. In the suburb of Fordsburg, where they settled, the houses were made of tin and were very uncomfortable. Ruth's father, Julius, soon lost interest in his Jewish background. He began to attend meetings held by socialists* like David Ivon Jones and Bill Andrews and joined the International Socialist League. In 1921 Julius and his wife, Tilly, became founder members of the Communist Party of South Africa (CPSA). Two years later Julius was elected chairperson of the Johannesburg branch. So when Ruth was born her parents were deeply involved in left-wing politics.

Johannesburg during the 1913 miners' strike – a scene Ruth's grandparents might have been familiar with

Ruth was a very active child, always asking questions. When she was at pre-school she started a library for her classmates. But they wouldn't read the books and she became angry. She told her mother, "If they don't read they'll never know anything." One day, when Ruth was four years old, her parents were late fetching her from school. She just jumped on a bus and arrived home by herself! And this is how she was all her life: confident and independent.

Ruth went to the Jewish government school in Doornfontein. Here she met Adele Bernstein, who remembered Ruth as a skinny girl in a navy gym and white shirt who wore her fuzzy hair short. Adele was the top student in English. But when Ruth arrived, she took over. "She put my nose out of joint," Adele remembers.

Ruth later moved to Barnato Park school where she made

friends with Myrtle Berman. Ruth and Myrtle discovered that they shared an interest in the Soviet Union. Both sets of parents talked about the Soviet Union often because they still considered it their "home". Soon Ruth invited her new friend home to meet her mother.

For most communists at the time, the Soviet Union was seen as a country in which the workers had won the battle for freedom. The way of life of people in the Soviet Union was seen as the goal all communists were working towards in their own countries.

Myrtle remembers that Tilly, Ruth's mother, talked to her for three hours non-stop about the history of socialism, the Russian Revolution, religion and other things. Myrtle never had to say a word. "My head was swimming with so many new ideas," she said. "But Tilly educated me. She formed my early political views."

In Ruth's home politics was always being discussed, especially the politics of the Soviet Union. According to Tilly the family didn't have ordinary friends, only people who were interested in politics. She said, "I didn't ever want anybody around who didn't understand what we were talking about."

When Ruth was 14 years old she joined the Left Book Club with Myrtle. The club had public debates and Ruth was excellent at these. She could stand up and talk about anything. She wasn't shy to talk in public. But in other ways Ruth was a very shy person.

Ruth's mother was very strong but not warm. Her father was quiet and often away at work. So Ruth's parents made it hard for her to be sure about her own feelings. She often thought she was ugly or that she was not as good as other people. So she covered up this insecurity by being very tough with other people. This made her seem rather scary. Only her close friends knew how unsure she was about herself.

But university was going to change all that. Ruth got a good matric pass and registered to do a degree in Social Science at the University of the Witwatersrand. There she was going to meet people with whom she felt safe and confident.

University, politics and journalism

At university Ruth met people who did not find her ideas strange. One of these was a law student called Ismael Meer, and they soon became romantically involved. Ismael rented a flat in Market Street, in central Johannesburg. It soon became a meeting place for radical* students like Nelson Mandela,

The University of the Witwatersrand, although it served mainly white students, provided a base for those opposed to apartheid

Anton Lembede, Oliver Tambo and Ruth. These people later became important planners of the Congress Alliance which united people of all colours against apartheid.

At university Ruth took a large number of courses. She was very good at studying. Her best subjects were English and African History and she scored first-class passes in six courses. But her great love at university was politics. Ruth and Ismael started an organisation called the Federation of Progressive Students. They were both elected to the Students' Representative Council (SRC) and they joined the Young Communist League (YCL).

As a student leader Ruth made a trip to a congress of students in Czechoslovakia and then travelled on from there to France, Hungary, Poland, Italy and Yugoslavia. In Yugoslavia she was taken on a tour to see how the ideas of socialism were helping people to re-build the country after the Second World War. The Yugoslavian peasants had fought against Hitler's German armies, and now they were working to bring about democracy after Hitler* had been defeated. This left a deep impression on Ruth.

Back in South Africa, Ruth also made a new friend called Joe Slovo. Her friendship with Ismael, who was of Indian descent, had been difficult because of apartheid. When they graduated from university and Ismael left for Durban, he and Ruth agreed to end the relationship.

Joe had been in the army. When the war was over he got a bursary and began studying at the University of the Witwatersrand. He and Ruth got to know each other in the Young Communist League. Joe came from a poor Jewish family which had emigrated from Russia. His mother had been a hawker and his father was a van driver in Johannesburg. Joe was forced to leave school early and work as a shop clerk. He remembers that Ruth was part of a university group in the YCL and he was part of a group of workers. He said, "We thought the university types were too big for their boots, so my first political conversation with Ruth was an argument! But we got over that." After returning from the war, Joe studied law at the

University of the Witwatersrand. In 1949 he and Ruth were married.

When Ruth completed her university degree she took a job with the Johannesburg City Council. But she hated it. She said, "I spent my days checking the figures for the number of play supervisors for white children in white parks, the number of beggars on the streets. The work bored and disgusted me."

In 1946 mine workers went on strike for higher wages and better working conditions. Ruth helped to produce pamphlets for the strikers. When the strike was over she left her City Council job and became a journalist. Although Ruth was only 21 years old, she had been very involved with the Communist Party and was known to be a good writer. She was given the important job of Transvaal editor with the socialist newspaper called the *Guardian*. The newspaper was a weekly that

The front page of the first edition of the Guardian, *19 February 1937*

specialised in news about politics and about workers. Its news from Europe was the best in South Africa. It almost always attacked the South African government over apartheid and exposed the terrible working and living conditions of black workers.

Ruth's new job on the *Guardian* was a big challenge. The newspaper had been started in 1937 by a group of socialists and was edited by Betty Radford. In the beginning it was very small. Betty remembers:

"The editorial office* was a desk in the corner of a store room at the print factory. We didn't have a typist or a messenger. And for some months we didn't even have a telephone."

During the war the *Guardian* became very popular because it had important news about the fighting, especially in the Soviet Union. By the end of the war 50 000 copies of the *Guardian* were sold every week. But even though it sold so well it was always poor. Companies were afraid to advertise in the newspaper because it was run by communists. They felt this would make people think they supported communism and would cause the police to harass them. So the *Guardian* had to rely on the money its readers gave it when they bought the paper.

The newspaper did many things to raise funds. Its staff would go knocking on people's doors asking for donations. Each week the paper would write appeals asking its readers for help. Its headlines read, "Help save the *Guardian*! We will close next week if we don't get money." The staff of the newspaper also ran Christmas clubs. Each week people would buy a Christmas Club stamp. Then at the end of the year they would get a big parcel of food for Christmas. But some of their money went to supporting the *Guardian*.

The newspaper also had lots of trouble with the government. The government would ban the paper. But the next week it would be out again, but with a new name. In this way it changed its name from the *Guardian* to *People's World*, then to the *Clarion, Advance, New Age* and finally *Spark*. The paper was banned five times, was bombed, spied on and had its presses sealed*. It was investigated by government commissions of inquiry. Most of its staff were arrested and many went on trial for high treason. Yet it came out every week for 25 years. It was the longest-running left-wing paper in South Africa's history.

When Ruth became Johannesburg Editor of the *Guardian* she was also joining an old tradition of liberation journalism*. Newspapers in this tradition had appeared during the French Revolution, in the early days of the English worker's movement, and in Russia.

The *Guardian* was very different to the commercial papers such as *The Star* and the *Rand Daily Mail*. These papers did not take black people seriously. The editor of the *Guardian*, Brian Bunting, accused the daily press of sticking its head in the sand like an ostrich. He said these papers seemed to think that the only people in South Africa were white. But the *Guardian* was interested in the political struggles of the oppressed people.

The *Guardian* reported about ANC meetings, police brutality and world events. It didn't treat its readers as if they were ignorant. ANC leader Walter Sisulu called the *Guardian* "an organiser of the oppressed and exploited people of our country". Women's leader Lillian Ngoyi said, "The *Guardian* is the only newspaper which fearlessly presents to the world the truth about the conditions of the oppressed people in South Africa." ANC activist Dr W. Conco wrote that it was the only paper which "breathes the spirit of liberation".

When Ruth joined the *Guardian*, socialist ideas were coming under attack from the government. But during the Second World War, which began in 1939, the Communist Party had become very popular. The Soviet Union's defence of the city of Stalingrad against the Nazi army was seen as the turning point in the war. The Soviet leader Stalin was regarded as a hero. Even "Ouma" Smuts, the wife of the South African Prime Minister, wrote a letter in which she said, "God bless Russia."

But after the war, governments in the West were afraid that the Soviet Union would help workers in their countries to rise up against the capitalist bosses and start revolutions in the

Western countries. In the United States, Canada, Australia, France, Belgium, India, Pakistan, Rhodesia and South Africa laws were passed against communists. In South Africa the executive of the Communist Party was put on trial in 1946 after a strike by mine workers for better wages. The government said the Party had organised the strike. The trial lasted four years before the accused were found not guilty.

The National Party had come to power in 1948. The new Nationalist government decided to ban the Communist Party. In 1950 it passed an Act of Parliament banning the Party, but just before the Act became law the Party dissolved itself.

Everyone thought that the *Guardian* would be banned as well. But it stayed alive for the time being. And Ruth, together with other journalists like Govan Mbeki, Brian Bunting and MP Naicker, used it to organise the oppressed people and to show how apartheid was making them suffer. Their journalism was different from reports in the commercial daily and weekly press. These newspapers only informed their readers. The *Guardian* didn't only inform readers, it urged them to take action. Its aim was to organise, educate and mobilise.

Soon after Ruth joined the *Guardian,* her friend the Reverend Michael Scott showed her an interesting report. It was about a court case in Bethal, where a potato farmer had been accused of ill-treating workers. She and Michael decided to go to Bethal to investigate.

What she found on the Bethal potato farms horrified her. She wrote: "The sort of thing that happens on these farms sounds like a story from the history of some ancient slave empire. Labourers are cursed, beaten, locked in their compounds at night. They have their clothes taken from them and savage dogs set over them in case they should try to escape."

Ruth found that workers were even beaten with whips and had their feet cut with hoes so they couldn't run away. Often they were chained together at night.

GUARDIAN

ELEVENTH YEAR, No. 26.   THURSDAY, JULY 3, 1941.   PRICE 1d.

THERE ARE MORE BETHALS
—*says* REV. SCOTT

JOHANNESBURG.—Exposures of the conditions of the Bethal contract farm labourers have created a sensation here, and throughout the country.

Statements issued by the Prime Minister's office, from Major van der Byl's bedside conference, have promised Cabinet and Native Affairs Department consideration. Newspapers' banner headlines indicate anxiety as to possible I.L.O. and U.N.O. repercussions.

The Rev. Michael Scott, interviewed by The Guardian this week, drew attention to certain disturbing features of the Bethal affair as taken up so vigorously by Johannesburg's daily and Sunday papers. "We must not be deluded into believing it is only in the Bethal area that near-slave conditions obtain. I have requests from many parts of the country to investigate the condition of farm labourers.

"It must be remembered that the State has all along continued to subsidise agriculture and in consequence also the exploitation of farm labourers.

"The Native Affairs Department has acquiesced in these conditions for over fifteen years. Through fear of losing the goodwill of the farmers it has even gone to the extent of appointing them on to committees to handle the distribution of the thousands of Africans arrested for offences under the pass and immigration laws.

"The Government has connived at the immigration of labourers from Nyasaland by issuing them temporary permits and then arresting these 'offenders' who, at the expiry of their contracts, do not succeed in finding work or in finding their way back to their homes. They are then deposited across the border and have to walk hundreds of miles back to their villages.

"THIS THE GOVERNMENT HAS KNOWN ALL ALONG."

The Rev. Scott emphasises that these conditions are in many respects worse than slavery. "In this century, after the Declaration of Rights has been signed, there are still human beings who are obliged to submit to such conditions in order to maintain themselves and their families.

"Let it be noted that there are no labour laws applying to agricultural workers and no trade unions to take up their cause."

Our Reporter Investigates

Last week The Guardian's Johannesburg reporter went to the Bethal district accompanied by the Reverend Michael Scott, to investigate conditions of farm workers and to follow up reports of ill-treatment amounting to slavery.

The Reverend Scott subsequently gave an interview to the Johannesburg daily press, and it has now been announced that General Smuts is personally taking charge of an investigation into the allegations of ill-treatment. Government interest is explained naively by the Cape Times in its front-page report on Monday: "The Government regards the matter as of the utmost significance, seeing that Native living conditions in the Union will be discussed at the September meeting of the U.N.O. General Assembly."

The Guardian *reports on the farm labour scandal in Bethal*

When she and Michael reported this in the newspaper it shocked the country. The Prime Minister said it was an embarrassment to the government and promised to stop it. But still it continued.

The Bethal farmers were very angry with Ruth and Michael. They invited them back to Bethal to explain what they had written. They wanted Michael to swear that he had lied in his reports to the *Rand Daily Mail*. Ruth and Michael went back to Bethal to meet the farmers, even though their friends said they were crazy. When they refused to say they had lied, the farmers threatened to kill them. They had to run for their lives.

Because many of the farm workers in Bethal were migrants, Ruth became interested in migrant labour*. She began digging for facts about migrant workers. She soon found that African people coming to South Africa looking for work were being stopped at the borders. They were told, "Either you work on the farms or you walk back home." Farmers were getting thousands of people as cheap labour in this way. More than 40 000 foreign workers were being used in Bethal alone.

But still the farmers wanted more workers. So the Government passed a law which said that if an African in a city had no job and no house he could be arrested. It became illegal to be unemployed! Police vans prowled the city streets on "pass raids". People who did not have passes to prove they had jobs were practically sold to farmers. Ruth wrote:

"Early each morning the pick-up vans drive up to the courts. They bring the men – and some women – picked up by the police raids the night before. Lining the streets outside the courts can be seen cars and lorries from the farms. From the maize and potato farms come the farmers looking for cheap labour. In a shed near the court Africans are pressed to accept farm work. The prisoners – none of whom have gone to court – are told if they accept farm work the charges against them will be withdrawn."

But with the assistance of ANC member Gert Sibande, Ruth helped the workers to fight back. Ruth and Gert exposed the brutal treatment of workers by the Bethal farmers. This encouraged workers to take the farmers to court and to bring criminal charges against their "bosses".

Ruth found that even children were being sold to farmers and these farmers were also building prisons on their farms so that they could use convicts as workers. In only one year – 1957 – nearly a quarter of a million prisoners were sent to these farm jails as labourers.

The government did not stop this brutality on the farms. Instead it banned the *Guardian*. But this fearless newspaper simply changed its name to *New Age* and continued to speak out against the cruelty on the farms. *New Age* demanded a commission of inquiry into farm labour. This demand was taken up by the ANC. Then in 1959 the ANC called for a boycott of potatoes. Many other organisations supported this call. The slogan for the boycott was, "We don't eat them." Thousands of people stopped buying potatoes and they began rotting in the markets and shops.

New Age *continued to publicise the farm labour scandal*

Soon after the boycott began, Ruth helped the wives of two missing workers bring a Heidelberg farmer called Potgieter to court. The judge, Justice de Wet, made a very important ruling. He said that the police had no right to sell people to farmers. He said that people who were arrested had to go to court or be released. They could not be sent to farms.

New Age reported the news of the judge's ruling with a big headline: FARM SLAVE SCHEME CRACKS! Two commissions of inquiry were appointed to look into farm labour – one by the government and the other by the Farmers' Union. Soon afterwards the government suspended forced labour. *New Age* journalists were very proud that they had beaten the government. They celebrated their victory with a headline: *NEW AGE* DID THIS!

Ruth had proved that journalists need not only report about the world. They could also change it. After Bethal, Ruth realised that writing could be a powerful political weapon. This was a lesson she was never to forget.

Building the Congress Alliance

4

The Communist Party dissolved itself in 1950 before the government could ban it. When this happened many people thought this was a trick. They thought the Communist Party would simply go underground. But it didn't. For nearly three years people who had been members of the Communist Party just waited, wondering what was happening. Ruth's friend, Hilda Watts, remembers:

"After a while when nothing happened, people began to talk to others. Little groups began forming in townships and in white suburbs. It was at that time that some people in Johannesburg decided, well, it's going to be dangerous, but we'd better get together and start a proper Party."

In the three years since the Party had dissolved many things in the country had changed. Radical members of the ANC Youth League, like the young Nelson Mandela, Oliver Tambo, Anton Lembede, Govan Mbeki and Walter Sisulu, had taken over leadership positions in the ANC.

In April 1952 the ANC's Defiance Campaign began. Africans walked through the "whites only" entrances of railway stations, rode in "whites only" lifts and sat on "whites only" benches. Thousands of people refused to carry passes and walked to police stations demanding to be arrested. Soon the prisons were overflowing. The government became desperate and imposed heavy sentences for defying the law.

The Campaign finally ended when police shot into a defiant crowd in Port Elizabeth, killing several people. But, because of the Campaign, thousands of people joined the ANC. It had become the most important liberation organisation in the country.

So when the communists began re-forming their Party, they had to take the power of the ANC into account. Communists held meetings around the country to discuss the way forward. These were called Discussion Clubs. Ruth was part of the Johannesburg Discussion Club, and club members began working out a strategy for the Party. These were people with a lot of political experience, like Moses Kotane, Michael Harmel, Govan Mbeki, Brian Bunting, Bram Fischer, Walter Sisulu, Joe Slovo and Ruth First.

After the Defiance Campaign, ANC leader ZK Matthews called on democratic whites to join the liberation struggle. In 1953 meetings were held at Darragh Hall in Johannesburg to discuss this call. Liberals and communists were all there and arguments broke out between them. When it came to support for black liberation, the whites could not agree on exactly how this support should be given. After the meetings some whites formed the Liberal Party, others secretly formed the South African Communist Party (SACP). And plans began to start the South African Congress of Democrats (SACOD). This new Congress had a number of communists in it and it had people with other political ideas as well. SACOD was formed as a home for whites who wanted to be part of the Congress Alliance, and it soon joined this Alliance alongside the ANC, the Indian Congress and the Coloured People's Congress.

Ruth was at the Darragh Hall meetings and she was a founder member of the SACP. She was also elected on the executive of SACOD. This was a very busy time for her. She had two small children, Shawn and Gillian, and gave birth to a third daughter, Robyn, in 1953. She was a full-time journalist and she was deeply involved with the political movement. Ruth was lucky that her mother, Tilly, was always there to help with the children.

In SACOD, Ruth and Joe joined the great planning meeting for the Congress of the People. The idea of a gathering to discuss a "people's parliament" and a Bill of Rights was first suggested by ZK Matthews.

As planning began, the idea of a Bill of Rights began to be

ONWARD to the CONGRESS of the PEOPLE!

We the people of South Africa, both black and white, have an urgent task to perform...

We are called upon to set down in writing those things which we would like to enjoy. ... below is won.

Yes, let us now set up the goal posts which are our objectives !

Let us speak together of Freedom !

Hereunder are some demands that have been sent in for inclusion in the....

FREEDOM CHARTER.

We Demand...

- Votes for all South Africans, both black and white.
- Higher wages and better working conditions.
- Better homes and housing for all.
- Land for the landless people.
- Free and compulsory education for all children irrespective of race, colour or creed.

What are your Demands...

If you are a FARMER what are your demands? _____

If you are a worker on a farm, what are your demands? _____

If you are a WORKER IN A FACTORY, what are your demands? _____

If you are a TEACHER what are your demands? _____

If you are a STUDENT, what are your demands? _____

If you are a PREACHER, what are your demands? _____

If you are a MOTHER, what are your demands? _____

If you are a BUS OWNER, what are your demands? _____

If you are a BUSINESSMAN, what are your demands? _____

This form was used by activists to collect the demands of the people

even more important than a "people's parliament". This bill was later to be called the Freedom Charter.

The date for the Congress of the People was set for June 1955. At this time, the Congress Alliance called on people and organisations to send in their ideas for a Freedom Charter. Thousands of ideas began pouring in – on bits of paper, old envelopes, notebooks . . . All over the country, ANC volunteers knocked on doors and addressed meetings. They asked, "What are your demands in a new South Africa?" And they wrote down the answers. In the cities people wanted good jobs and good schooling for their children. They wanted to own their houses. They did not want the government to forcibly remove them from their homes.

In the rural areas people wanted different things. They didn't want their cattle to be killed by the government. They wanted more land. Some men even said they wanted more wives. Almost everyone wanted passes to be abolished and prison labour to be stopped. Sometimes a person would tell the volunteers, "Look here, I'm not a politician, don't ask me." But the volunteers would ask, "Are you happy staying in this small room? Do you like passes? Are you happy that your children get a bad education?" Then the person would say, "No, I'm not happy," and start to remember all the things he or she wanted changed. And the volunteers would write them down.

To collect all these ideas into a single document a Drafting

Committee was formed, and Ruth was asked to join it. Because she was the only journalist on the committee, she was given the task of sorting out all the ideas and combining them into a single document. So the first draft of the Freedom Charter was drawn up by Ruth.

The great gathering of the Congress of the People was held at Kliptown near Johannesburg on 25 June. The 3 000 delegates representing the oppressed of South Africa approved the Charter by voting on each clause. But such an event could not carry on without the police. They surrounded the meeting on the second day and confiscated all documents. They said they were investigating acts of treason.

NATS TERRIFIED BY FREEDOM CHARTER
INSIDE STORY OF POLICE RAIDS

The Nationalist government's response to the Freedom Charter campaign, as reported in the headlines of New Age.

Ruth could not attend the Congress. A few weeks earlier the government banned her. This prevented her from attending any political meeting. But it did not stop her journalism or her secret work with the Communist Party. She became a tireless worker for the causes of SACOD and the Congress Alliance.

However, her work was not going unnoticed by the police. As Ruth and her family were about to leave for their Christmas holiday in December 1956, she and Joe were arrested and taken to the Fort, Johannesburg's main prison. They joined 154 other people in prison on a charge of attempting to overthrow the state by force. The charge was high treason.

The case dragged on for four years. It was the longest political trial in South African history and was a terrible time for the accused and their families and friends. But in many ways the government had done the Congress Alliance a favour. It united the leaders of its opposition under a single roof. The 156 people charged were in some ways a "parliament of the people". They were African, Indian, "coloured" and white. There were liberals, churchmen, communists and nationalists. They were all crowded together day after day in a special court. Here they not only defended themselves from the state's accusations but also talked, and planned a future non-racial South Africa.

Ruth and Joe, together with the other accused, were let out on bail. Nearly every day they had to drive to Pretoria to be at the court case. This made life very difficult. But in the end they won. They were found not guilty. However, by then the government had declared a State of Emergency* and the ANC and Pan African Congress (PAC) were banned. But that part of the story comes later.

Ruth First with other treason trialists: from left to right, J Nkampeni, Farid Ahmed and Joseph Morolong

5

Battle of the passes

At the centre of all Ruth's political struggles was her journalism. She used her writing to fight against apartheid and to change people's lives. We can see how Ruth did this if we look at her fight against passes for African women.

The government was afraid that African people would flood into the cities. They made laws to keep them out. The Group Areas Act forced people to live in townships and other laws made people live in "bantustans". But the most cruel laws were the pass laws. These laws were passed in the 1950s when all African men were forced to carry a pass book. If a policeman looked in this book he could see everything about a man. He could find out who he was, where he lived, where he worked and even whether he had ever gone to jail. If the pass book showed that the man was not allowed to be in the city then the policeman could lock him up.

Front page of New Age, *14 November 1957, reporting on more Group Areas legislation*

People hated the pass which they called the "dompas" or "stinka". The journalist Lewis Nkosi wrote bitterly about this in 1959. He said:

"I do not live apart from my own reference book (pass) any more. In fact I have decided I AM THE REFERENCE BOOK! It stands for my personality. It defines my character. It defines the extent of my freedom. It has become my face. What began as a system purporting to smooth my efforts to earn a living and move about with proof of my claim to the citizenship of this country has now completely taken me over."

But these feelings did not bother the government at all and in the early 1950s, the government said it wanted African women to carry passes as well. The authorities had tried to do this in the Orange Free State in 1913 and it had led to riots. In the 1950s the new Nationalist government decided to try again. They said that when women came to cities they brought their whole family and this filled up the cities. If women carried passes then the government could control their movements into the cities.

Women decided to form an organisation to fight the laws. The Federation of South African Women (FEDSAW) was started in 1954. Men in the ANC were not too happy about their women becoming political fighters. But at the first FEDSAW conference a woman stood up and said, "If the men stand in our way we shall sweep them aside for our rights." She said that men had already lost the battle over passes and it was now up to the women to take up the fight.

A year after it began, FEDSAW organised a protest march of 2 000 women to the Union Buildings in Pretoria. They demanded an end to passes. Ruth was with the women and her heart was stirred by the sight of hundreds of women demanding their rights. She wrote in *New Age*:

"Pretoria was conquered by women! The women came from all parts of South Africa. For hours they poured up the steps of the Union Buildings and congregated in the concourses while their leaders attempted to deliver their protest. THE CABINET MINISTERS RAN AWAY FROM THEM – SO THE WOMEN

LEFT THE PETITION ON THEIR DOORSTEP. When the leaders returned and reported that the protests had been delivered the women rose to sing *Inkosi Sikelele iAfrika* and the sound and harmony rang out from the tiers of women."

After this demonstration Ruth began to help build the women's pass campaign. She used her newspaper to announce anti-pass campaigns and marches, and reported on them when they happened. The government began issuing passes to women in small rural towns, hoping FEDSAW would not notice. But Ruth followed the government pass units there and reported about this in her newspaper.

Women became angry when the government tried to trick them in this way and thousands of women who had taken passes burned them. The government was furious. Ruth wrote that the women should not be afraid and that they should fight and be proud. She helped African women to think about themselves in a different way.

But the government was determined that women should carry passes. So on 9 August 1956 FEDSAW called for another

From left to right: Lilian Ngoyi, Helen Joseph and Sophie Williams, delivering petitions against the pass laws to the Prime Minister on 9 August 1956, when 20 000 women protestors marched to Pretoria

march on the Union Buildings. This time 20 000 women came. They travelled from all over South Africa. Many arrived with babies on their backs. In Pretoria they filled the trains and buses. The men stepped back to let them pass. They said, "The women are marching for our freedom." Lilian Ngoyi, Helen Joseph, Rahima Moosa and Sophie Williams took the thousands of signed petitions to the door of the Prime Minister. But he was not in. The women said, "He has run away from the women." The petition said:

"We are women from every part of South Africa. We are women of every race, we come as women united in our purpose to save the African women from the degradation of passes. We African women know too well the effect of this law upon our homes, our children. We will not rest until all pass laws and all forms of permits restricting our freedom have been abolished. We shall not rest until we have won for our children their fundamental rights of freedom, justice and security."

When the women had handed in the petitions they waited in silence for half an hour. They sang together, "Strijdom, you have tampered with the women, you have struck a rock." The government was shocked at the numbers of women, and delayed issuing passes to women. It was a great victory.

But the government never forgot its idea of passes for women. In 1958 pass units began registering domestic servants in the white Johannesburg suburbs. They posted letters to white "madams" telling them to send their "native domestic servants" to the Commissioner's offices to get passes. *New Age* and FEDSAW began organising against the government plan. In one of the biggest headlines ever to appear in *New Age*, Ruth wrote: "JO'BURG WOMEN SAY NO TO PASSES." She reported on a march by women from Sophiatown to the Commissioner's office in Johannesburg. Nearly 2 000 women were arrested, and Ruth wrote that the jails were "overflowing with the women and their children". She wrote:

"African men handed over their pants to the women. The women were the strong ones. They were beaten and herded into police vans singing a new song with the words: The enemy of the African is the pass." She said that in the main Johannesburg prison, the Fort, there was "no space left even for a rat".

The Johannesburg newspaper, *The Star*, was not very interested in the beatings. It reported the arrests to its white readers with the headline, "No nannies today." The next day it told its worried readers, "No servants? Why, it's easy to do without them."

Still the women burned passes. Ruth reported pass burning all over the Transvaal. In Zeerust, in the western Transvaal, she exposed terrible police brutality. A woman told her:

"We have been murdered because of passes. Machine guns have been used against the people. I have seen people being shot. Men have been handcuffed hands and feet. I have escaped from the hell at Zeerust. But there are still those in this hell who stand firm against passes." The government responded to Ruth's reporting by declaring a State of Emergency in Zeerust and banning all newspapers from the area.

By this time the pass had become the most powerful symbol of opposition to the Nationalist government. In Natal in 1959 women took action, fighting against passes. In Cato Manor women attacked police with sticks and drove them off. Police retaliated by beating and arresting hundreds of women.

In 1963 the government eventually made passes compulsory for African women. They had been trying to do this since 1913! But although African women eventually lost their battle, they had changed their opinions about themselves. They realised that they could become political fighters like their men. Ruth's reporting was very important in this change of ideas. She had shown the women how to connect with each other across the land to fight for their rights. A woman in Natal said:

"The government forced us to take off our head-doeks to be photographed for passes. It was against our custom but we had to do it. The light got into our brains. We woke up and saw the light. And the women have been demonstrating ever since."

Azikwelwa – we will not ride

6

Ruth was a Marxist* writer and this made her interested in the problems of poor people. From the time the Second World War began in 1939, thousands of people had come into Johannesburg looking for work. When they could not find houses they rented rooms for their families. When there were no more rooms left they built shacks out of tin and boxes. Ruth was very concerned about how people had to live in these townships.

Ruth First at a Human Rights Day meeting in Alexandra, 1952. With her are, from left to right, Yusuf Cachalia, Walter Sisulu and Albertina Sisulu

Her investigation into township conditions began in the freezing winter of 1951. That winter the Johannesburg City Council doubled the rents in all its townships. The Council was so cruel that even the white manager of "Non-European Affairs" resigned in protest. Ruth swung into action. She said that if the city needed money it should tax the rich and not the poor. She said:

"Placing new burdens on the Africans – the city's poorest, hardest hit by the cost of living, at the lowest end of the cost of living allowance scale, the most fleeced* by profiteers and black-marketeers in every shortage, carrying the heaviest burden of transport fares because they are pushed into the furthest locations – can only cause trouble."

She wrote that the rent increase would leave no money over for bus fares and said worker transport should be subsidised*. Over the next few years Ruth's view of the South African economy was so different from that of the government and big business that it seemed as if they were talking about different countries.

In 1956 the Standard Bank reported "outstanding industrial growth" and claimed "new record levels" in farming, mining, power and transport industries. The bank said the amount of money everyone was earning was rising fast. The government reported record sales in most industries and in farming. It boasted that living standards were rising.

But Ruth saw a different picture. South Africa, she said, was drifting into crisis. She said that although conditions were getting better for whites, they were getting worse for Africans. She calculated that each African family in Johannesburg needed R34 a month to live. But she found that most were earning only R24 a month. Between 1944 and 1951 food prices had nearly doubled and each African family had to spend R8 in every R10 on food. She said crime was going to rise and there was going to be a struggle around the transport services.

She was quite correct. The protests began in Alexandra, a crowded township near the rich northern suburbs of Johannesburg. It had become a place of poverty and crime,

BUS BOYCOTT STILL SOLID

Amazing Demonstration Of People's Unity

NEW AGE

Vol. 3, No. 13   Registered at the G.P.O. as a newspaper.

NORTHERN EDITION   Thursday, January 17, 1957   PRICE 3d.

JOHANNESBURG

AFTER one week — including a furious rainstorm on Friday — Johannesburg's vast African townships of Alexandra and Sophiatown, Pretoria's Lady Selborne and Mooiplaas remain 100 per cent solid in their boycott of the monopoly Public Utility Transport Company's bus services, against the penny increase in fares.

Western Native Township, with an eighty per cent effective boycott, and Atteridgeville, Pretoria, are not far behind. With hundreds of buses standing idle or running "skeleton services", PUTCO's losses have been estimated at between two to four thousands pounds a day.

THIS IS ONE OF THE MOST REMARKABLE ILLUSTRATIONS OF AFRICAN SOLIDARITY EVER TO BE WITNESSED IN THIS COUNTRY.

The Transportation Board has threatened to prosecute employers who send the firm's transport to fetch and return workers, and the traffic department ceaselessly hunts down temporary "pirate" taxis. Though the Alexandra Taxi Owners' Association is co-operating handsomely — they have decided to cut fares from 2s. 6d. to 1s. 6d. for the duration — and hundreds of European car owners make a daily practice of stopping to give lifts to tired workers, the great majority of the boycotters continue to walk — eight miles from Sophiatown, eighteen from Alexandra — to and from work every day. They rise before the summer sun has risen, and when they get home it is dark again.
(Continued on page 6)

A cart stops to give a group of African women a lift. Others continue on the long march to town, day in, day out, rain or shine, determined not to pay the 1d. increase in bus fares.

MAYIBUYE! SAYS THE RABBI

PORT ELIZABETH.

When the New Age interviewed Rabbi Dr. Andre Ungar on January 5, the eve of his departure from the Union, he said he would sum up his thoughts and wishes about South Africa in one word:

"MAYIBUYE!"

Dr. Ungar, who wore an A.N.C. brooch on the lapel of his coat, left P.E. by air on his way to England where he is going to settle after his deportation from South Africa.

TREASON TRIAL A POLITICAL PLOT, SAYS DEFENCE

THE ACCUSED ALSO WALK

Five of the treason trial accused join the bus boycotters each morning and walk the nine miles from Alexandra township into Johannesburg to take their places in the dock. Here are Mr. Stephen Dhlamini of Durban, and Mr. S. Masemola, Mr. P. Nene, Mr. James Hadebe and Mr. Alfred Hutchinson, all of Alexandra township.

GOVT. AIM TO OUTLAW OPPOSITION

● THE TREASON TRIAL IS A POLITICAL PLOT BY THE GOVERNMENT OF THE TYPE WHICH CHARACTERISED THE PERIOD OF THE INQUISITION AND THE REICHSTAG FIRE TRIAL.

● It is an attempt to silence and outlaw the ideas held by the 156 accused and the thousands whom they represent.

● It reflects a battle of ideas : on the one side the ideas of equal opportunities and freedom of thought and expression for all; on the other side those which deny to all but a few the riches of life both material and spiritual.

These are some of the points made by Mr. V. C. Berrange, one of the defence counsel, when the preparatory examination on charges of treason was resumed at the Johannesburg Drill Hall last week. He was replying to the general outline of the Crown case presented by the Prosecutor, Mr. Van Niekerk, before Mr. Wessel, the Magistrate, adjourned the case for the Christmas recess.

Mr. Berrange summarised the general allegations of the Prosecutor under four main heads:—
1. That the various organisations mentioned by the Prosecutor as forming the national liberation movement decided to convene the Congress of the People to adopt the Freedom Charter, envisaging a radically new form of Government for South Africa;
2. That the change to the new form of Government would be brought about by force;
3. That outside countries or influences...
(Continued on page 3)

DEFENCE FUND NOW REGISTERED
—See page 2

New Age *reports on the Alexandra bus boycott of 1957*

but it was soon to become a place of hope and struggle as well. In January 1957 the Public Utility Transport Corporation (PUTCO) decided to raise its bus fares from fourpence to fivepence. The people of the Reef immediately refused to ride the buses and voted to walk to work and back. They united behind a slogan: *Azikwelwa* – "We will not ride". Ruth reported the first day of the boycott:

"The streets were strangely quiet. First the great lumbering green buses came . . . empty. Then over the rise that obscures Alexandra Township from the main road came the eruption of workers in the dawn hours when mists and brazier fires mingle indistinguishably together. End to end the road was filled with shadowy, hurrying figures. Then the forms thinned out as the younger men with the firmest, sprightly step drew away from the older people, the women, the lame. Later . . . the same crowds turned their backs on the city and again took to the roads. Down the hill the foot-sloggers found it easier . . . the spindly-legged youngsters trotted now and then to keep up, the progress of the weary women was slower still, here a large Monday washing bundle carried on the head, there a paraffin tin, or a baby tied securely to the back. In pelting rain, running the gauntlet of police patrols, the boycotters walked on."

The government announced it would smash the boycott. Police took this as an order to make trouble for the boycotters. They stopped people in cars from giving the walkers a lift. They banned taxis in the area. They arrested hundreds of people for crossing against the traffic lights at 6 o'clock in the morning when there was very little traffic. And they raided Alexandra, which was the most defiant boycott area, and arrested nearly 15 000 people for minor offences.

The government and the commercial newspapers blamed communists and the ANC for the boycott. But a new form of organisation was running the boycott in Alexandra. The leaders were from little, local grassroots committees with names like the Alexandra Smallholders' Committee and the Vigilance Committee.

These committees came from the people of Alexandra and not from the established political organisations, many of whose leaders were involved with the Treason Trial. The committees attacked the government and the City Council. They were even critical of the ANC leaders, who they said were good at talking but not good about taking action to help the boycotters:

"The ANC leaders are from time to time the main anti-boycott spokesmen. A struggle properly conducted – a struggle in which the interests of the people are placed FIRST – above the individual leader – above self-importance – above organisations – such a struggle will always expose quislings* in our midst. We must take note. A man in the police uniform is easy to spot, but a man dressed in strong talk and weak actions – has to be DISCOVERED through his actions. This is the case with the ANC."

Ruth realised that this was a new form of political struggle. Ordinary working class people were becoming politically aware. She wrote:

"African workers are no longer bewildered, mute and tribal. The boycott has shown that they are industrialised, politically aware, articulate and purposeful. Their organisations are mature. They have shown that amazing ability to communicate and organise without an organisation."

In the end the boycotters won. The fares were kept at fourpence. By then each worker in Alexandra had walked more than 4 000 kilometres!

The Alexandra bus boycott was to change Ruth's ideas about political struggle. It taught her to believe in the political understandings of ordinary working people. This belief remained with her for the rest of her life.

7 Friendship and *Fighting Talk*

At times the struggle for freedom was very exciting. But the official policy of the government was apartheid, and people fighting to break down apartheid had many problems with the authorities. White South African anti-apartheid activists experienced many problems from conservative and right-wing whites. Ruth wrote that white activists, fighting alongside Africans, Indians and "coloureds", led an increasingly dangerous life.

"Our consciences were clear," she wrote. But as the years went by these whites lived in two worlds which seemed to be moving away from each other. "We had the good living that white privilege bought," she said. "But at the same time we were involved in revolutionary politics which was against white privilege." And as the struggle became fiercer, white privilege no longer protected people like Ruth from the anger of the Nationalist government.

In the 1950s this group of whites numbered about 200 people, most of them connected to the Communist Party or the Congress of Democrats. The Communist Party was a very secret organisation. It was made up of "cells" which were connected through key people across the country. Many people within the Party took up important positions in the ANC and the Congress of Democrats. They were a tough bunch of political fighters. But as their politics became known within white society, they became social outcasts. Neighbours noticed that "blacks" were always visiting their houses in the white suburbs. These activists had parties and meetings which were raided by the police and reported in the press. The children of white activists also had trouble from other children at school, especially when their parents were arrested or their photos appeared in newspapers in connection with the Treason Trial.

So the white fighters for freedom in their white suburbs became islands of non-racism, with dreams their neighbours couldn't understand. But they made up for this isolation with good parties. Ruth's 21st birthday celebration and her wedding were big non-racial affairs.

In October 1958, when part of the State's case against the people accused in the Treason Trial collapsed, the Slovos held a huge celebration at their home in Roosevelt Park. At about 10 pm the police raided the house and a photographer from *Die Vaderland* jumped through a window and took pictures. The police carried away all the liquor, but the party continued.

The next day the photographs of the party were in *Die Vaderland* and its readers were shocked to see whites and blacks dancing together. Ruth was really angry, not so much about the raid as about the reporter crashing in on her party. She laid a charge against him for illegal entry. But no record of whether she won or lost the case can be found.

Another way in which sections of the Congress movement created a special bond with each other was through its press. A publication which caught the mood of the non-racial leadership was a journal called *Fighting Talk*.

The journal was started by an organisation called the Springbok Legion during the Second World War and was written for soldiers. The Legion was one of the founding organisations of the Congress of Democrats. So when this Congress was born, it was decided to continue *Fighting Talk* under an independent board. In 1955 Ruth was appointed editor.

This extra job was a challenge for Ruth. She was not paid for doing the job, and she had to work long hours every month to put the journal together. But as editor, she could control what went into *Fighting Talk* and she decided to create a "journal for thinking democrats of all races".

Like the *Guardian*, *Fighting Talk* was always short of money.

For this reason, much of Ruth's time was taken up trying to find donations and reminding people to pay their subscriptions. But she was very persuasive, and people like Nelson Mandela, Oliver Tambo, Moses Kotane, Michael Harmel, Albert Lutuli, ZK Matthews, Govan Mbeki, Yusuf Dadoo, Jomo Kenyatta, Kwame Nkrumah and Julius Nyerere were soon writing articles for her.

She would argue with contributors, tell them what to say, and demand stories on time. She wrote to Lionel Forman saying, "PLEASE, PLEASE, PLEASE . . . Write pronto*. And in English, not gibberish!" Lionel was a great friend of Ruth's. He was a lawyer and a clever political writer. He often helped to edit the communist newspapers and was one of the 156 people charged in the 1956 Treason Trial. He often teased her about her nagging. He once wrote:

> There was a young liberal called Ruth,
> An absolute stranger to truth,
> Whose temper was bad.
> (I know it – By Gad)
> A temper most sadly uncouth.

Ruth used *Fighting Talk* to fight passes, police brutality and poor labour conditions, and to support bus boycotts, the Freedom Charter and the Congress movement. But she also used it to challenge readers to think. Many years later, the *Guardian* editor Brian Bunting said:

"Ruth had the capacity to dig out facts and talent, to harness not only her own energies but also those of others. Nor was she content merely to propagandise or sloganise. She believed the best propaganda was the facts, and editors and readers knew they could rely on every word she wrote. Nothing was left to chance, nor was any stone left unturned. She worried and worried at a problem until it was solved."

When the State of Emergency was declared early in 1960, *Fighting Talk* could not come out for six months. Ruth wrote:

"In the countrywide swoops in which 2 000 South Africans of all races were rounded up and detained, *Fighting Talk* lost writers, readers, editorial and circulation staff, sales agents and our most staunch supporters."

When it started up again after the Emergency, *Fighting Talk* had a new focus. It tried to introduce South Africans to the culture and politics of the rest of Africa. But in doing this, it also introduced its readers to the politics of liberation and armed struggle taking place in the rest of the continent.

8

Towards new horizons

In 1960 police shot and killed people in Sharpeville and Langa who were demonstrating against passes. As people buried their dead after the police shootings, a terrible anger spread across the land. In Cape Town the Pan African Congress (PAC) took over the townships of Langa and Nyanga. PAC members blocked the roads and stopped police from getting in. More than 30 000 people, led by the brave young student Philip Kgosana, marched into the centre of the city. The leader of the ANC, Chief Albert Luthuli, called for a day of mourning and a worker stay-at-home.

The Sharpeville shootings in which 69 people were killed caused shock and disgust throughout the world. The United States condemned the shootings and the United Nations asked why unarmed people, protesting against passes, had been shot in the back. Foreigners who had invested money in South Africa began to panic. They all took their money out of the country, and in six months more than R12 000 million left South Africa. The Pretoria government thought a revolution was about to happen. It declared a State of Emergency, which allowed the army to rule South Africa. Thousands of people were arrested and imprisoned without trial.

Political activists knew that the arrests were coming. They planned a signal system to warn each other. Rica Hodgson remembers being phoned by Nelson Mandela. She said:

"He gave me a message which was gobbledygook*. So I immediately wrote it out. When my husband, Jack, came back I gave him the message and he said: Oh my God, that means arrests. I must go and warn people." Congress leaders talked about going into hiding or staying visible. Joe Slovo said he had important legal work to do and was not prepared to "disappear". He was soon arrested and spent six months in jail.

Ruth decided to go into hiding. She dyed her hair red, packed her children into the car, and drove to Swaziland. She found many other South Africans there. She and the girls moved into a flat with another family in Mbabane and they began their first experience of exile. Ruth's daughter Robyn, who was eight years old at the time, remembers: "It was tense but fun, though none of us really knew what was going on. It was at times also very fearful. But mostly I remembered Ruth's red hair!"

Before the emergency was over, Ruth secretly returned to Johannesburg and went into hiding. It is possible that she came back to take part in talks about whether the Communist Party should stop being a secret organisation and make itself known to the public. At these meetings, Michael Harmel argued that: "You have to say something as a communist. You have to talk about socialism and marxism, and you can't do that in the liberation movement. You have to speak in your own right. And you can't say after the revolution: Hey, by the way, we're also here and we want power." So the Party decided to become known by publishing a leaflet saying the South African Communist Party existed. It caused a big stir in the press.

When *New Age* began printing again after the Emergency, Ruth was back at her desk. But South Africa was a very different place to what it was before the Emergency. It was dangerous to oppose the government. It was also very hard for her to be a journalist in a country where human rights had disappeared. She wrote that only in South Africa was the government marching backwards into the past. Instead of talking to people it was tear-gassing them. Instead of giving them the vote it was using guns against them. Instead of uniting the country it was appointing its own chiefs and cutting up the country into bantustans

But government repression did not stop her writing. It just changed the way she wrote and what she wrote about. Instead of writing weekly newspaper stories she turned to deeper investigations. In this way she began collecting material for her first book.

This is how it happened. For years her old friend Michael Scott, the priest, had been fighting to force South Africa to free Namibia (then called South West Africa). After the First World War, South Africa had been asked by the League of Nations to rule the territory until it could govern itself. But the South African government did not want to let it go. Michael started fighting for Namibian freedom at the United Nations in the early 1940s. But by the 1960s the territory was still being ruled by South Africa.

Ruth decided that Michael's fight should be taken forward. Her plan was to interview the people of Namibia and to publish their views and opinions about their country's future in a book. In 1961 she drove to Namibia, taking all the back roads to avoid the ever suspicious police. She slipped quietly into Windhoek and booked into a hotel.

For four days the Special Branch of the police didn't realise she was in Windhoek. Then they woke up with a jerk. The detectives began to follow her. She wrote:

"They wore shorts and rugby socks. They worked in pairs and padded along six paces behind me, smiling stupidly when I caught their eye. The trail to the dry-cleaner and the shoemaker, the skulking* next to the telephone booth, both ends of the road and every exit of the hotel patrolled, detectives following me to the airport, watching me at breakfast, interviewing people I had seen."

Ruth talked to people on street corners, in cars, under trees, in crowded shops. Some people were afraid to be seen with her because of the policemen who were always near. She expected to be arrested, but the government waited until she got back home to Johannesburg. Moments after she arrived, two policemen banged on her door. They had a banning order which forced her to stay in Johannesburg and made it illegal for her to talk to other banned people.

The banning stopped Ruth's journalism. She wrote:

"I could take part in no further exposés of forced labour like my work on Bethal. I could no longer enter African townships, so I could no longer personally establish the contacts of African men and women who tipped me off about some new vicious scheme of the police and administration. I could not attend meetings, so other people had to take the notes and the photographs for me. I couldn't write anything for publication, so I had to sit at my desk and check other people's writing instead. Working with these bans, and always being watched by the Special Branch, was like going to work in a mine field."

But the ban didn't stop her from typing. So she got together all her information about Namibia and began writing her book. It is easy to think that this writing was easy for her. But in fact it was a big struggle. She had never written anything so big before. One of her closest friends, Ronald Segal, said:

"Many good journalists cannot make the jump from the article to the book. They are at home in the sentence and the paragraph, but they lose their way in the larger landscape. Ruth was aware of this. Some people, who saw how confident she was, never knew the nervousness with which she approached her work."

Nevertheless, in quite a short time, she had finished. The book told the terrible history of colonialism in Namibia. The people of the country, she wrote, were heroic swordsmen on horseback in an age when war was being fought by machines and guns. They only wanted more grazing land but against them were all the armed powers of western Europe. The politicians wanted treaties. The industrialists wanted to mine. The missionaries offered them bibles but wanted their souls.

These people became "handcuffed by slips of paper" and were shipped off to the farms and mines as cheap labour. She wrote:

"They must have permits to seek work, permits to be in the area for any purpose other than to seek work, service contracts to prove that they are working, passes to prove that they are schoolboys and too young to carry passes, certificates of registration allowing residence in the area, permits to travel, tax receipts. Passes and permits are their licence to live."

Of course she could not publish such a book in South Africa. Her typewritten pages were smuggled out of the country and were published in London in 1963. Important critics and historians praised the book. They called it "journalism of the highest kind". But the book was banned in South Africa, and if someone was found with a copy they could be sent to jail for five years. The government was furious. It served two more banning orders on Ruth. She was banned from almost everything connected to journalism. From this point her days as a journalist in South Africa were over.

By now Ruth and her family were under a lot of political pressure from the police. Joe's legal practice was suffering and the children were becoming bewildered by secret meetings and the attentions of the police. The three girls were not kept informed about the activities of their parents. Joe remembers that they were becoming isolated from their friends and their families. He said:

"The girls had no support at school. When a black kid's parents were arrested other kids thought they were heroes of the struggle. But when a white parent was arrested other white kids called them a communist and a traitor. It was so hard for them. They suffered more than black kids in this respect." But before we find out what happened to Ruth and her family, we need to look at the other political events with which Ruth was involved while she was writing the book.

Armed struggle and Rivonia

9

Many years of marches, protests and boycotts had come to nothing. All the government had done was to ban, jail and harass people who had reasonable demands. After the Government declared a State of Emergency and banned the ANC and PAC, the African people had been faced with two choices. They could submit or they could fight: these were the words of Nelson Mandela. A group within the Congress Alliance decided to fight.

This leadership faced a difficult task. In 1961, when the decision to fight was taken secretly, many leaders were banned, in exile or in jail. But they set themselves the task of convincing their followers that open revolt had to be used against the state because passive resistance had failed. And they began to study the possibilities of such action.

There was a strong feeling among many leaders of the ANC and Communist Party that the State of Emergency, imposed after the Sharpeville shootings, was a sign of government weakness. When *New Age* began publishing again after the State of Emergency was lifted, it ran a headline which said: "Freedom is within our grasp." It wrote:

"The oppressed peoples of South Africa are on the march, and not all the savagery of the Verwoerd government can prevent their ultimate victory. The Emergency proved one thing to all our peoples – THAT LIBERATION IS NEAR. There is no longer any question of whether freedom will come. It is only a question of when and how."

At the end of 1960 the Communist Party held a national conference. This conference instructed its Central Committee (of which Ruth was a member) to work out a plan of action. The conference also called for "economic sabotage as the first stage to guerrilla warfare". Six months later underground activists, including members of the Communist Party, formed Umkhonto weSizwe, a people's army, which began training for acts of sabotage.

Nelson Mandela said later that the Congress leadership was forced to start Umkhonto. This was because people were so angry about the Sharpeville killings that they were about to turn to disorganised terrorism. Other sabotage groups began forming at the same time. These were the National Committee of Liberation (which later became the African Resistance Movement), the Trotskyist Yu Chi Chan Club (YCCC) and Poqo, the military wing of the Pan African Congress.

As a journalist, Ruth began to set the climate for the change of strategy from peaceful protest to armed sabotage. Her articles in *New Age* and *Fighting Talk*, as well as articles she got other people to write, now talked about the liberation movements in the rest of Africa. *Fighting Talk*, she said, would focus on "the front lines of the battle to free Africa".

Ruth also started to look at the possibilities for armed resistance in South Africa. She wrote a series of articles in *Fighting Talk* on "alternative" South African history, which she said was "a tribute to the men and women of all races who are bringing a new life and a new nation to birth before our eyes". She wrote, "We are in sight of freedom in our lifetime. We live in the presence of history."

During this time Ruth also began helping Govan Mbeki to finish his book about the Transkei called *The Peasants' Revolt*. Govan was a member of the ANC, and a man with deep roots in rural Transkei. He said that peasants had always thought along military lines and that they would be a force for liberation. He began writing the book secretly in Port Elizabeth. But when he had nearly finished the rough draft, he was arrested and held in prison for five months. This didn't stop him writing, however. He managed to find a pencil and wrote on toilet paper. But he started the book all over again. The rolls of paper were smuggled out of the prison and Ruth was called in to help. She began to put the two versions of the book together and get it ready for publication.

On his release from prison Govan was banned. As Ruth was also banned it was illegal for them to meet. But they met anyway, in secret. Then Govan was arrested again, and Ruth wrote most of the last chapter and sent the book to England for publication.

The Peasants' Revolt had a big influence on Umkhonto weSizwe. It said the peasants were ready for armed struggle. Govan wrote about the Mountain Committee in Pondoland. This committee had horses and knives and a few guns, but it defied the government, even though the government had armoured cars and aeroplanes. It formed an army of brave men on the hills. He wrote:

"The march through Bizana, when an old man carrying a black flag at half-mast led a procession of 5 000 peasants without any experience of mass forms of pressure, must be one of the greatest feats of organisational ability that the liberation movement and the oppressed people of this country have so far accomplished."

For Ruth, the time after Sharpeville was very busy but also very frightening. She was a member of an illegal organisation and was being asked constantly to write pamphlets and articles. ANC leader Walter Sisulu said Ruth was, "one of the most dynamic personalities in the movement. She was moving in the circles of the ANC, the Indian Congress, the trade unions; and as editor of *New Age* in Johannesburg she was central to nearly everything."

But being central meant that she and other Congress leaders were well known to the Security Police. They were spied on, their telephones were tapped and their post was opened. It was a time of terrible tension and Ruth's nerves were on edge. Congress members were being jailed or going into exile. And those who stayed were becoming more isolated because people were scared that if they visited a Congress activist the police would harass them.

By 1963 *Fighting Talk* had gone too far for the Nationalist government. Ruth knew its end was coming. She was defiant. "*Fighting Talk* has always been the voice of the fighters with weapons or with words," she said. Speaking about the Congress leadership, she wrote:

"We will try to match our actions to our talk over these many years. We are confident that in this way lies victory for our ideas. Perhaps not now. Perhaps not for some time to come. But in the end it must be so. In the end of ends, it is not the government of this country which will crush the people; but the people who will crush the government."

But the life of Congress publications inside South Africa was clearly over. The Congress of Democrats was banned in September 1962 and two months later *New Age* was told it had to close. Then in March 1963, in terms of the "gagging clause" of the new Sabotage Act, both *Spark* (the successor to *New Age*) and *Fighting Talk* were forced to stop publication. All their writers, including Ruth, were prevented by law from writing for any publication whatsoever.

Then, on 11 July 1963, a baker's van drove slowly into the grounds of Lilliesleaf Farm in Rivonia near Johannesburg. The farm was one of the secret meeting places of Umkhonto weSizwe. Policemen burst from the back of the van and surrounded the house. Everyone on the property was arrested. By pure chance, neither Ruth nor her husband, Joe, were at the farm. Ruth had been there a few hours earlier, and Joe was overseas organising support for Umkhonto.

After the raids, police began arresting people all over South Africa and preparing charges of treason against the Umkhonto High Command. This was to lead to the so-called Rivonia Trial. The arrests were to halt Umkhonto's sabotage campaign for more than ten years. Ruth was so central to the resistance movement that she knew the police would want to question her. They followed her by day and watched her by night. She knew it was just a matter of time before they detained her.

She had enrolled in a course for librarians at Wits University. On 9 August 1963, as she walked out of the university library, two men walked up to her.

Ruth said:

"Though I'd never seen them, they looked like what we took to be caricatures* of Special Branch men. They were very tall, very gangly. They had very badly fitting suits with baggy trousers and big feet. They didn't say an awful lot:

'We are from the police.'

'Yes, I know.'

'Come with us please. Colonel Klindt wants to see you.'

'Am I under arrest?'

'Yes.'

'What law?'

'Ninety days . . .' "

Under the "90 Days" law, a person could be locked up in prison for three months without being charged for any crime. The police took Ruth to her home and searched it for two hours. Then they took her to the police station. Ruth remembered:

"The largest of my escorts carried my suitcase into the 'Europeans Only' entrance. As he reached the charge office doorway he looked upwards. 'Bye-bye, blue sky,' he said, and chuckled at his joke."

Ruth Slovo is to be charged

RUTH SLOVO, mother of three children, who was detained for 90 days on 9 August, is to be charged – probably at the end of her 90-day period next week.

Mrs. Slovo was transferred from Marshall Square to Pretoria at the beginning of this month. Her husband, Mr. Joe Slovo, and her father, Mr. Julius First, have both fled South Africa.

Yesterday, Mrs. Slovo's mother, 65-year-old Mrs. Matilda First, was told by Col. J.G. Klindt that Mrs. Slovo would be brought back to Johannesburg next week.

Mrs. First said last night that Colonel P.J. Venter had told her about a fortnight ago that her daughter would eventually be charged. He did not say what the charge would be.

Mrs. First is caring for the three Slovo children aged nine to thirteen.

A tiny column in the Rand Daily Mail *gives an idea of the results of Ruth's detention on her family*

44

10

Alone in a prison cell in Marshall Square police station, Ruth suddenly realised something she had not thought of before. There was no doubt that she knew a lot about the underground movement. And as a journalist her job had been to gather information and give it to those who wanted it. But to do what came so naturally to her, to give information when her audience was the Security Branch, would be to betray her comrades. And this she could not do. She sat worrying about this in her dark, dirty cell:

"What did they know? Had someone talked? Would their questions give me any clue? How could I parry the interrogation sessions and find out what *I* wanted to know, without giving them the impression that I was resolutely determined to tell them nothing? I had to find a way not to answer questions, but without saying explicitly to my interrogators, 'I won't tell you anything.' "

As the days became weeks of solitary confinement, this worry was to turn into a crisis. The Security Police were no longer the uneducated Afrikaners of the early 1950s. They had studied security work and they were clever and cruel. They told her: "We're not holding you. You're holding yourself. You have the key to your release. Answer our questions, tell us all we want to know, and you will turn the key in the door. Make a statement and in no time you will be back with your children."

For the first two months of imprisonment nothing much happened. Ruth remembered that she kept fighting. She said, "I was a lot of trouble to the police." But then the Special Branch began to put on the pressure. They said, "You're an

Ruth with her daughters Robyn and Gillian

obstinate woman, Mrs Slovo. But remember this. Everyone cracks sooner or later. It's our job to find the cracking point. We'll find yours." Then they asked, "What were you doing at Rivonia?"

Soon after this, the police let her know that they were investigating her father, her mother and her brother. Her whole family was being pulled into the line of fire. She said this "froze my limbs":

"The children had lost Joe in June, me at the beginning of August. My father might well be in hiding. I had left the children with heartache but I had the comfort of my mother as a substitute. If she was taken, they would be abandoned."

After two months Ruth was moved to Pretoria Central Prison. The Marshall Square cells were dirty and noisy, but they were somehow more human. Pretoria Central was bright and polished and so isolated it could have been on the moon. This depressed Ruth terribly. She said:

"I grew increasingly subdued. My imprisonment was an abandonment in time. I felt alien and excluded. I was without human contact and exchange. No echoes reached me. I was suspended in limbo, unknowing, unreached."

Then, during a visit, her mother whispered to her some terrible news. Bruno Mtolo, a cadre central to the Umkhonto High Command, was talking to the police. He knew a lot about Ruth's involvement in the underground, and his testimony would put an end to her hopes of release. She said:

"I felt as though I had been poised on a high diving board above a stretch of water, when someone had suddenly pushed me. And in the hurtle downwards the water below had dried up."

Then another shock came. "Your 90 days is up," said the police. "We're releasing you." Ruth couldn't believe it. And the police took her back to Marshall Square and booked her out. She walked down the street in a daze, her suitcase in her hand, looking for a public telephone. She was free.

Suddenly two detectives walked up to her and said, "You're under arrest. Another 90 days." So two minutes after her release Ruth was back in her cell, shocked and emotionally exhausted. She became desperate for human contact. She found she was even prepared to talk to the detectives. When they asked her if she would make a statement she just said "yes".

But in the interrogation room Ruth realised she was in terrible trouble. The detectives did not ask her questions. They just said, "Tell us everything. Start at the beginning." Ruth began to tell the story of her life and political involvement, trying not to give away any important information. But she was too exhausted to work out what was important and what the police knew. She said:

"There was no time to wriggle, to fabricate, to gauge reaction, to probe, to find out anything for myself. I was breaking down my own resistance. It was madness for me to think I could protect myself in a session like this, in any session with them. I had no idea what they knew, what contradictory information they had wrenched from someone else. They were giving nothing away; they were becoming too experienced for that."

When Ruth hesitated, one of her interrogators, Swanepoel, screamed at her, "I know you communists by now. And I've learned that they have to be put up against a wall and squeezed, pushed and squeezed, into a corner. Then they change, and talk." Ruth felt her last bit of strength draining out of her body. She refused to continue with the statement but she felt broken.

Soon afterwards her mother, Tilly, was granted a visit. She whispered the last thing Ruth wanted to hear, "We're depending on you."

Ruth felt the whole weight of the Congress movement bearing down on her. The statement was hanging over her like doom. She felt she had betrayed her comrades when they most needed her to be strong. She wrote a farewell note to Joe in the back of the Bible in her cell and swallowed a whole bottle of sleeping pills her doctor had left her.

Fortunately, the dose of pills was not enough to kill her. When she woke up she was in a state of shock, and her cries and weeping echoed through the police station. When a doctor was called, Ruth said to him, "Am I heading for a nervous breakdown?" He said, "You've already had one."

Over the next few weeks Ruth slowly recovered. The shock of the attempted suicide stopped any further thoughts about killing herself. But she now found that instead of wanting to be released, she was afraid to be. Her cell was a place of security. The outside world was full of people she felt she had betrayed. When a Security Branch detective came with her release papers she refused to believe him. But this time it was for real. The detective offered to drive her home. She said, "When they left me at my own house at last I was convinced that it was not the end, that they would come again."

When Ruth arrived home, her mother and daughters were shocked at how she looked. The youngest daughter, Robyn, said, "She looked absolutely terrible. I was horrified at the state of her and the fact that she seemed to have lost power." Ruth found it hard to be with people or to run the house. Her friend Hilda Watts took the girls on holiday. And Ruth began a slow recovery with the help of close friends like Barney Simon and Moira Forajz.

But Ruth's time in South Africa was clearly coming to an end. She could no longer be a journalist. Joe was in England and was not able to return to Johannesburg because he would be arrested. The Rivonia Trial was going against the Umkhonto leadership and most of them would get life imprisonment sentences. It was only a matter of time before Ruth would be arrested again.

Sadly, she decided to go into exile. The decision to leave South Africa was greeted with delight by Ruth's daughters.

Ruth Slovo and her children quit S. Africa for good

By MARGARET SMITH

MRS. RUTH SLOVO, former treason trialist and 90-day detainee, left Jan Smuts Airport, Johannesburg, for Europe last night on an exit permit. This means she will not be allowed to return to South Africa.

Mrs. Slovo was arrested in August last year and held for 117 days in solitary confinement at Marshall Square, Johannesburg, and in Pretoria Central Jail.

She left last night with her two younger daughters, Gillian, 12, and Robyn, 10. The third daughter, Shawn, aged 14, left South Africa earlier this week by ship.

A number of Security Branch policemen were present at the airport when she left.

Friends said the family was going to London to join Mr. Joe Slovo, the Johannesburg advocate who escaped from South Afri.. tn June last year. They said that Mrs. Slovo had not wanted to leave South Africa permanently. But her application for a passport, was refused and an exit permit was granted a few days ago.

"The various bans and restric-

tions imposed on Mrs. Slovo made it impossible for her to continue living in South Africa," a friend said yesterday.

Ruth Slovo, a journalist and author, was forbidden to write and barred from entering premises connected with printing or publishing or to assist in any way with the dissemination of news. Nothing she said could be quoted and she could not write for overseas publications.

Mrs. Slovo was formerly Johannesburg editor of New Age and later, when this newspaper was banned, of Spark. The prohibition of its entire staff from having anything to do with newspapers forced its closure.

When she could no longer work as a journalist, Mrs. Slovo started a post-graduate course in librarianship. It was while she was working at the library of the University of the Witwatersrand in August last year that she was

arrested and detained under the 90-day law.

At the end of 90 days, she was taken from her cell and told that she was free.

Rearrested

Ruth Slovo then walked out of Marshall Square police station on to the pavement outside. She was looking in her handbag for a tickey to make a telephone call to her children when she was rearrested.

While she was under detention, a warrant was issued for the arrest of her father, 70-year-old Mr. Julius First—described by the police as "South Africa's most wanted political figure." Despite watches at the borders, Mr. First escaped and is now overseas.

Ruth First's brother, Ronnie, was also arrested under the 90-day law and held in solitary confinement for three weeks. At the end of this time police told him they did not believe that he was involved in suspicious political activities.

MRS. RUTH SLOVO, former 90-day detainee, left South Africa last night on an exit permit.

The Sunday Times *reports on Ruth First leaving South Africa for London on an exit permit*

They couldn't wait to leave Johannesburg. The tension had become too much for them. Robyn remembered, "I just wanted to get out of here as quickly as possible. I didn't have any friends."

Her classmates at school – many of whom had been critical of her parents' support for black liberation – gave her a Zulu doll as a farewell present. This was not a gesture of goodwill on the part of her classmates. They chose the Zulu doll to show their disapproval of anyone who supported the struggle for black liberation. This was just too much for the 10 year old, "I smashed it against a pole on the way home," Robyn said. On the day of her departure Ruth wrote a brief, sad note to her friend Sadie Forman:

"My dear Sadie
Have to say goodbye. Wretched! But must make the best of it. Will try to. Love you all. Ruth."

On 14 March 1964, Ruth and two of her daughters, Gillian and Robyn, boarded a plane at Jan Smuts Airport. Ruth did not know it at the time, but it would be the last time she would ever see South Africa again.

11 Into exile

When the plane touched down at Heathrow Airport in London, Ruth, Gillian and Robyn stepped into a new, free world. Joe was there to meet them. Shawn was to join them later.

But Ruth carried with her two heavy burdens. One burden was that she felt that she had been defeated in detention. And the other was a feeling of responsibility over the collapse of the liberation movement in South Africa after the Rivonia Trial.

The family moved into a house in Camden Town and Ruth began dealing with the two problems in the way she knew best – by writing about them. Her spirit had been wounded by detention and she needed

Ruth First's arrival in London, as reported in the overseas media

Mrs. Ruth Slovo, who spent 117 days in detention under the 90-day law, is reunited with her husband, Mr. Joe Slovo, at the London Airport.

With them are their children, Robyn, 10, and Gillian, 12, who travelled with Mrs. Slovo.

Mr. Slovo last saw his wife when he fled from South Africa nine months ago. Mrs. Slovo, a jurnalist who wrote under the name of Ruth First, was released from custody in Johannesburg in December.

TITO ORDERED TO REST

BELGRADE. — President Tito of Yugoslavia has been ordered by his doctor to have medical treatment and a rest on Brioni Island, his residence in the northern Adriatic.

The Yugoslav State head, who will be 72 in May, has left Belgrade for Brioni. — SAPA-Reuter.

to get herself together again. Joe, together with her close friends Ronald Segal and Cecil Williams, begged her to write about her prison experiences. Ruth was a shy, private person. She had written thousands of words about other people, but writing about herself was hard. She protested that it was not important, but her friends said she needed to expose the cruelty of the South African regime. So slowly and painfully she began to write.

Her book *South West Africa* came out in 1963, and *117 Days* followed two years later. *117 Days* was to make her famous in Britain. She began writing with a sense of her own defeat at the hands of the Security Police, but by the time she had finished she had come to terms with her statement to the police and her attempted suicide. She wrote:

"I had been reeling towards a precipice and I had stopped myself at the edge. I had *not* been too late to beat them back. I had undermined my own resistance, yet I had not after all succumbed. In the depth of my agony I *had* won."

The cover of Ruth First's book, 117 Days

The book was an immediate success, and the British Broadcasting Corporation (BBC) asked if they could make a film about it with Ruth acting as herself. Could she go through all that again, even for a film? But writing the book had healed Ruth and she said yes.

She wrote the script and in 1966 the film, which was called *90 Days*, was finished. The South African ambassador in London tried to stop its screening, but the BBC ignored him and millions of people all over Britain saw the horror of solitary confinement in South Africa on their TV sets.

By the time the film was screened, Ruth had got into the swing of London. She loved the big city and its buzz of people. And she had three great passions which London provided for and which may have startled her communist colleagues. She loved good, expensive Italian shoes, elegant luggage and silk shirts. If she was going to live in exile, she decided, these would be her compensation.

But, mostly, Ruth spent time with her typewriter. Her daughters remembered that they would wake up early in the morning to the sound of Ruth tapping the typewriter keys. And at night they went to sleep to the same sound.

Her philosophy about any task was "to get stuck in", and when something needed to be finished she could work through the day and through much of the night as well. Her output was amazing.

In 1966 Ruth went to Nairobi to help former vice-president Oginga Odinga write a book about his political career. Because of Odinga's politics and Ruth's reputation, she was deported from Kenya with only 24 hours' notice. But she edited the book anyway, which was called *Not Yet Uhuru*.

During this time Ruth went on tours of Britain, giving public speeches against apartheid and talking to groups of people about detention and racial discrimination in South Africa. She also took part in campaigns for the Anti-Apartheid Movement and the ANC. But her writing never stopped. In 1967 she edited and published a second book on Namibia, as well as *No Easy Walk to Freedom* by Nelson Mandela, *The Peasants' Revolt*

Ruth First speaking at an anti-apartheid meeting at Trafalgar Square

by Govan Mbeki and the book on Odinga. She also organised a conference on Namibia held in Oxford.

As soon as these tasks were finished, she began trying to come to terms with the second burden she had brought over from South Africa. But by now her questions had gone much wider than the setback to the Congress Alliance in South Africa.

She wanted to know about colonialism and the governments which followed it. Why had so many African freedom fighters failed to maintain democratic governments once they came to power? Why were so many African states such as Ghana, Nigeria, Uganda and Libya ruled by the military?

She was not afraid to ask hard, unpopular questions. Her research took her to Ghana, Nigeria and Sudan. And she began to write a book which was an honest look at the failures of decolonisation in Africa. This was called *The Barrel of a Gun*. Why, she asked, had so many governments in Africa come about by a seizure of power by arms – by coup d'état? Coups, she said, were the result of a "failure of politics". She wrote:

"There has been clever and endless talk about politics, side by side with the gaping poverty of political thought . . . Politicians are men who compete with one another for power, not men who use power to confront their country's problems."

But her work on military regimes did not make Ruth lose her faith in democracy and socialism. When the book came out it was described as one of the best books ever written about Africa. Reviewing the book, political writer Ralph Milliband said:

"She was never disillusioned. She never gave the slightest hint of doubt about the justice of her cause or about the urgent need to strive for its advancement. She criticised the shortcomings, stupidities and crimes of her own side. But this never stopped her believing that there was a struggle to be fought against the monstrous tyranny that is South Africa. Beyond all setbacks, it was her hatred of oppression which moved her."

By now Ruth was a skilled writer and a well-known political journalist in Britain. In 1972 she was given a research post at Manchester University and taught on the sociology of rebellion in post-colonial Africa. During this time she did research for a book on Colonel Gadaffi in Libya. This came out in 1974 and was called *Libya, the Elusive Revolution*. She also did work for the United Nations Commission on Human Rights. And all the time her writing was getting better.

In 1973 Ruth was offered a post as lecturer at Durham University. This would mean that she would have to live away from her home in London during the week and come home by train at weekends. It was difficult for her family, but the girls were grown up and Joe was often away on political work. Ruth was always modest about her achievements and she was flattered by the offer. The work would be exciting and she decided to take the job.

She was a good lecturer and soon became a favourite with the students. History writer Gavin Williams, who attended one of her lectures, said:

"I was struck by the fact that academics don't lecture like that. They're used to taking their audiences for granted. Ruth didn't. She grew up with political audiences on the Johannesburg City Hall steps and the need to get her argument across. Very few lecturers at Durham were as good as she was."

At Durham University two new directions opened up for Ruth. One was feminism, and the other was Mozambique. In South Africa, Ruth was very much in a man's world of politics and journalism. But in London she found the value of close women friends. She wrote to her friend Miriam Hepner, "I've found several women here whose company I have grown to prefer because they are invariably better to talk to than men."

At Durham she introduced a course on women's studies and became very sensitive to "gender" issues. Her close friend Rica Hodgson remembers how her husband, Jack, once told a sexist joke in front of Ruth. Rica said:

"She slammed Jack for that, really laid into him. He didn't know what the problem was. But he went and read some books about feminism. And he never made a joke about women again!"

At a feminist meeting once, people were praising the Soviet Union for the way it treated women. They said it was different to England. There, women were doctors and engineers and they were equal to men. But Ruth jumped up. People thought she would agree, but she asked, "In the Soviet government, with all those men in their double-breasted suits, where are the women? Only when I see them there I'll say sexism is dead in Moscow."

During her work at Durham, Ruth met a younger researcher called Anne Scott and they decided to work together on a book about the nineteenth century South African novelist, Olive Schreiner. In many ways, Olive was very like Ruth. Both were women ahead of their time. Both had struggled against racial and sexual discrimination and both had suffered for their political views. The book, *Olive Schreiner,* was beautifully written and was praised for its sensitivity and accuracy. Ruth, in her modest way, wrote that "for once I feel something I have written is quite good."

Also while she was teaching at Durham, Ruth spent time away teaching at Dar es Salaam and at Maputo in Mozambique. These trips made her long to go back to South Africa. When she was offered a job as Director of Research at the Centre for African Studies at the Eduardo Mondlane University in Maputo she jumped at it. It would be the nearest thing to coming home.

Joy and tragedy

In newly independent Mozambique, Ruth found a country struggling out of a colonial past towards socialism. For years Mozambique had been ruled by Portuguese colonists. They had used the country and its people to make themselves and Portugal rich.

But the Mozambicans remained poor and oppressed. They worked on the farms and in the mines of South Africa and were badly paid. Their children were given very little education and often went hungry. So people like Eduardo Mondlane and Samora Machel formed a guerilla army and an organisation called Frelimo to fight the Portuguese and win their freedom.

After years of fighting, Frelimo forced Portugal to give up Mozambique. After freedom was won there was still poverty. But there was hope. For Ruth there was also the warm Indian Ocean, the beautiful and quiet beaches and the gently waving palm trees of her beloved Africa. In *The Barrel of a Gun*, she had said, "I count myself an African and there is no cause I hold dearer."

The capital city of Maputo is small, and Ruth soon became involved with the politicians and planners of the new, independent country. In many ways her work at the Eduardo Mondlane University brought together all her previous skills. Her work was about how to solve the problems of poverty and food production as well as labour and planning. It was work which was needed and which mattered.

Ruth set up a nice little flat in the city and soon had many friends and contacts. She seemed to relax – she allowed her hair to become frizzy again and wore more comfortable clothes.

She was back home at last, and getting closer to what was going on in South Africa.

At the Centre for African Studies she saw, as one of her main jobs, the training of Mozambicans in research and policy planning. She taught students and researchers how to combine their ideas and their studies with political commitment. But because of the lack of trained staff she and the few other researchers were kept very busy. One week Ruth would be flying to Sweden to negotiate for funds. The next week she would be paying the woman who made the Centre's tea.

Soon research work at the Centre began to be respected. Ruth's team was described as "a group of very good Marxist academics driven by an excellent investigative journalist". Staff at the Centre published studies on the tea and cotton industries, and then began working on one of the most difficult problems in Mozambique – migrant labour. The government was very interested in this work. They consulted Ruth often to ask her help with their planning.

Each year thousands of peasants would travel to the Rand to work on the mines. Mozambique and its people needed the money they earned, but they did not like the way their country depended on South Africa. Then the mines decided to cut back on the recruitment of Mozambican miners. This was to cause terrible hardship. The Maputo government needed help to decide what to do.

Ruth and her team went to work on the problem. They interviewed hundreds of mine workers and visited their farms and villages. They collected songs, history and stories. Their findings were eventually published as a book called *Black Gold: The Mozambican Miner.*

However, Maputo was very close to South Africa and the South African regime was known to target exiled activists for assassination. Joe was worried about Ruth. He wrote, "Take precautions. Never open the door if you don't know who is on the other side and be careful with your post . . ."

But high security wasn't Ruth's style. She was a public, open person. She said, "You can't run an academic institution like that." Ruth was receiving hundreds of letters a day – huge piles from all over the world. Anyway, she was more worried about Joe. By then he was head of Umkhonto weSizwe and an obvious target. It never occurred to Ruth that South African agents would also be interested in her.

But Ruth was doing important work which could harm South Africa's interests in the region. Ruth did not trust the South African government and was against any deals between independent African countries and apartheid South Africa. And her views were taken seriously in Maputo.

Ruth First with ANC President Oliver Tambo and President Samora Machel of Mozambique

Then two events happened which may have made her a target for the South Africans. The head of Mozambican state security suddenly defected to South Africa. He knew Ruth's views and he also knew how little she worried about security. And soon afterwards Pretoria began negotiations which were to bring about the Nkomati Accord, a treaty between South Africa and

Mozambique. Nkomati was the place where the treaty was signed by the leader of South Africa, P W Botha, and President Samora Machel of Mozambique.

The accord was a non-aggression pact; both countries agreed that they would not allow their territories to be bases for attacks against each other. What this actually meant was that Pretoria was becoming more and more worried that Mozambique was being used as a base for Umkhonto attacks against South Africa.

But Maputo was a strong supporter of the ANC. So why did its leaders sign the Nkomati Accord? During the Zimbabwean war of independence, the white Rhodesian government had helped to set up a group called Renamo which opposed the elected Mozambican government. When Zimbabwe became independent, South Africa continued support for Renamo, which waged war against the Frelimo government in Maputo.

Bit by bit, this civil war weakened the Maputo government. The South African government knew this, and it waited for the right moment. Then, in 1984, a terrible drought hit the region. Thousands of refugees from the drought and the war were flooding into Maputo. The Pretoria government also knew that Mozambique depended on the money which was being brought back home by Mozambican labourers working on the South African mines. It could threaten to stop these workers coming into South Africa, and it used this as a lever to bargain with Mozambique. So when the South African Foreign Minister went to ask President Samora Machel to sign a non-aggression treaty, Machel was forced to sign. Ruth would have fought against the signing with all her might.

But this was not to be. Before the treaty was signed, Ruth was killed instantly when a letter bomb exploded in her hands. Africa was robbed of one of its most powerful planners. Just as had happened so many years ago when she was released from prison after the Rivonia arrests, "they" had come again.

In a police bar in Pretoria two years later, Captain Dirk Coetzee, commander of a "Death Squad", told *Rapport* newspaper reporter Jacques Pauw that after the killing, South African spy Craig Williamson had told Coetzee, "We got First". The plan, Coetzee told Pauw, had been made at a police-owned farm called Daisy. He said that the unit ordered to kill Ruth was Section A of the Security Police under Brigadier Piet Goosen, the man who had interrogated Steve Biko.

On the farm, said Jacques Pauw, Goosen and his colleagues made the bomb and put it in an envelope stolen five years earlier from the United Nations High Commission for Refugees in Swaziland. After the bomb exploded, Coetzee said it was a time of joy for the police. He said, "The men drank beer and brandy and Coke and patted each other on the back. They all agreed they had dealt the enemy a terrific blow."

But across the land Ruth loved, millions of people knew they had lost a valuable leader. Mourning services were held throughout South Africa. A trust was formed in her name.

This trust was made up of a group of Ruth's close friends and relations who wanted to honour her name. They collected many of her books and writings and also raised money to support people who needed financial assistance to study and undertake research.

In 1992, after the ANC and Communist Party were unbanned, an award in Ruth's name was started for investigative journalism. The first person to win it was a young journalist who had uncovered links between the South African Defence Force and the killing of Eastern Cape leader Matthew Goniwe.

Ruth would have wished for no better monument.

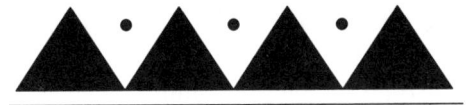

Learn new words

caricatures: when certain characteristics of people are exaggerated (page 44)

editorial office: the place where items for a newspaper are prepared and put together in preparation for printing the paper (page 9)

fleeced: exploited, taken advantage of. (The woolly coat of a sheep is called a "fleece": it is taken from the sheep by people for their own use. This is why the verb "fleece" is sometimes used to mean taking advantage of somebody or exploiting them. (page 27)

gobbledygook: nonsense (page 35)

Hitler, Adolf: the leader of Germany from 1933 to 1945. He believed that the Germans were the most superior race in the world. He tried to conquer Europe, and his actions led to the beginning of the Second World War. Hitler's beliefs and policies led to the killing of many millions of people throughout Europe. (page 7)

instruments: tools (page 2)

liberation journalism: investigation into and reporting about issues which are important to the liberation struggle (page 10)

Marxist: a word describing someone who believes in the philosophy of Karl Marx, the man who (together with Friedrich Engels) wrote some of the most important books about socialism (page 26)

migrant labour: a situation where many of the workers for certain unpopular jobs (usually hard and dirty ones) come from outside the country (page 13)

pogroms: large-scale organised killing of one group of people by another group of people (page 3)

presses sealed: the government locked up the place where the printing presses were and did not allow the newspaper to be printed (page 9)

quislings: traitors to the struggle who are working with the enemy (page 30)

radical: with views very different to those held by most people around them (page 6)

skulking: hiding oneself, especially for an evil purpose (page 37)

socialist: someone who believes in an economic system in which the masses of the people own the "means of production" – that is, the factories and the land and so on. The political system based on this belief existed in the Soviet Union from 1917 to 1989 and was called **socialism.** (page 4)

State of Emergency: a situation where the government says that it has the authority to give the police and sometimes the army powers against people that they do not usually have (page 20)

subsidised: part of the cost is paid for by the government (page 27)

Activities

1

Choose the correct answer

(1) Ruth First's grandparents came to South Africa from
(a) Switzerland.
(b) Israel.
(c) Russia.

(2) What political organisation did Ruth First's parents help to start in 1921 in Johannesburg?
(a) The Socialist International.
(b) African National Congress.
(c) The Communist Party of South Africa.

(3) At university Ruth helped start the
(a) NUSAS.
(b) Federation of Progressive Students.
(c) Club for Gender Equality.

(4) After Ruth left her job with the Johannesburg City Council she began a new job with a newspaper called
(a) *Rand Daily Mail.*
(b) *New Nation.*
(c) *Guardian.*

(5) The *Guardian* newspaper was started by
(a) businessmen.
(b) the government.
(c) a group of socialists.

2

Make your own drama

Read the report about a play based on the life of Ruth First, that was staged in London. Then read the last part of Chapter 9 which tells you about Ruth's arrest under the "90 Days" law. Create a 15 minute drama of Ruth's meeting with the security police as she walked out of the university library.

You can extend this activity and make a model of the stage set and a poster advertising the play.

For more background information read, *The jail diary of Albie Sachs*, by A Sachs and see the film or video, *A World Apart*, which was based on the life of Ruth First. The filmscript was written by Ruth's daughter, Shawn Slovo.

Ruth First story a tour de force on London stage

HERALD CORRESPONDENT

LONDON—In the glut of plays and programmes about South Africa on at the moment in London, a small but powerful production called "117 Days" has emerged on the West End's fringe.

An adaptation of banned journalist Ruth First's autobiography, it grittily covers Miss First's imprisonment under 90-day detention in 1963 when the wife of advocate Joe Slovo and friend of Walter Sisulu and Nelson Mandela spent 117 days in solitary confinement.

A play of only 55 minutes length, it's a one-woman tour de force performance by an actress of Egyptian-American origins – with a remarkable likeness to the young Miss First – called Tamar Brown.

Concentrating on the mental and emotional helplessness of a prisoner with a battle to fight far beyond the daily regime of sanity, Miss Brown's intense performance manages to be coloured by touching mundane reactions and a certain sense of ironic humour as she works her way through each day, punctuated only by more questioning and chalking up another notch on the proverbial bedpole, in her case, the cell's chair.

"117 Days" started life on stage when Miss Brown first read the book after hearing about Ruth First from her father who had met the Johannesburg-born political activist. She contacted the First family and Ruth First's friends overseas and with playwright Nikki Foulds started the adaptation.

Interview Ruth First

Ruth First was a committed political activist and investigative journalist who worked hard to bring about change in South Africa. Imagine you are a newspaper or television reporter. Write or act out an interview with Ruth First that takes place during her exile in Mozambique. Some of the questions you ask her could include the following:

(i)   What pressures does her work put on her as a woman and a mother?
(ii) What dangers does she face?
(iii) Why did she choose to oppose apartheid?
(iv) What does she think and feel about the position of women in South Africa?

Discuss and debate

Discuss in small groups what your thoughts are about children who feel "neglected" when their parents are actively committed to bring about change in the world outside their home.

You could screen the video of the film, *A World Apart*, based on the life of Ruth First, to provoke discussion.

Books about the life and times of Ruth First

Bernstein, H. 1967 *The world that was ours.* London: Heinemann.

Davenport, T.R.H. 1977 *South Africa: A modern history.* London: Macmillan.

First, R. 1988 ed. *117 Days.* London: Bloomsbury.

First, R. 1970 *The Barrel of a Gun: Political Power in Africa and the Coup d'Etat.* London: Allen Lane.

First, R. 1975 *Libya: The Elusive Revolution.* London: Penguin.

First, R. and Scott, A. 1980 *Olive Schreiner.* London: Andre Deutsch.

Forman, S. and Odendaal, A. 1992 *A trumpet from the housetops.* Cape Town: David Philip.

Joseph, H. 1986 *Side by side.* London: Zed.

Lerumo, A. 1980 ed. *Fifty fighting years: The South African Communist Party 1921–1971.* London: Inkululeko Publications.

Mandela, N. 1987 ed. *No easy walk to freedom.* London: Heinemann.

Mbeki, G. 1991 *The prison writings of Govan Mbeki.* London: James Curry.

Pampallis, J. 1991 *Foundations of the new South Africa.* Cape Town: Maskew Miller Longman and Zed.

Sachs, A. 1990 *The jail diary of Albie Sachs.* Cape Town: David Philip.

Slovo, G. 1989 *Ties of blood.* London: Headline.

Wells, J. 1991 *We have done with pleading: The women's 1913 anti-pass campaign.* Johannesburg: Ravan Press.